1. Edition 2021
ISBN Paperback: 978-3-949304-10-1
ISBN Hardcover: 978-3-949304-11-8

Dear Parents and Little Explorers,

this book comes with a <u>free</u> digital bonus which contains the **zoo soundscapes** accompanying the story plus **fun coloring pages**.

Ask your parents to download this <u>free</u> bonus at:

www.jolaswittler.com/zoo

Your friend,
Jolas

We live in a beautiful world.
May our kids have fun learning about it.

Let's begin the journey!

Hello and welcome to the zoo!
This visit will be fun for you!
You'll see some animals for sure.
Let's not waste time and start the tour!

ZOO

ZOO

First, we meet the elephant up close!
He has big ears. The trunk's his nose.
He got some fruit. He'll eat them all,
when he is done with playing ball.

The tigress is a big, striped cat.
Her cubs are tiny. Look at that!
She's lying quietly on the shore.
But when she's angry, she will roar!

As you can see, giraffes are tall.
Compared to them, we are so small.
Just look at those long necks they've got!
Hey, can you see the heart-shaped spot?

The ostrich is a special bird,
the tallest one, but what's absurd:
He'll never get to reach the sky,
as he runs fast but cannot fly.

Let's go inside the petting zoo.
With donkeys, goats, and ponies, too.
Stay calm, as there's no need for fear.
It's safe to gently pet them here.

The time has come to take a break.
Let's play together near the lake.
Let's have a drink and eat a snack,
and soon we will be back on track.

Say, have you met our sea lions yet?
Their home is icy cold and wet.
Just watch one gets his favorite dish.
Who wouldn't love some yummy fish?

The penguins love to jump about,
into the water and back out.
They catch the keeper's fish — Snap! Snap!
Don't spoil the polar bear's long nap!

The turtle is relaxed and cool.
It crawls and swims inside the pool.
It is protected very well,
because it lives inside a shell.

The sloth is very calm and slow.
He does not make a giant show.
You see him hanging in a tree.
Now count his fingers: one, two, three.

Koala bears are gray and small.
Surprise! They are not bears at all!
They're chewing eucalyptus leaves.
Say, can you see one in the trees?

This friend is special to this zoo.
All day he munches on bamboo.
Which animal could be so rare?
You're right, it is a panda bear.

The sun goes down like every day.
And we had so much fun to play.
But now it's time to leave the zoo,
as it prepares for nighttime, too.

ZOO

And when it's getting dark at night,
the baby owl hugs mom so tight.
She shuts her eyes and rests her head
like every child at home in bed.

There is a map of the zoo.
Did you spot every animal? Do you know their names?

ZOO

Did you notice?

1.) Can you find every animal from this list? Which sounds do they make?

2.) Have you spotted these scenes? Where are they happening?

3.) There is a raven in every picture! Did you spot them all?

Bonus Offer

We have a special gift for you!

Ask your parents to download the "Animals of the Zoo" activity pack containing the accompanying **soundscapes** and cute **coloring pages** for <u>free</u>!

www.jolaswittler.com/animals

Thank you for reading this book!
If you enjoyed it, we would be so
grateful for an online review.

Does your kid love trucks?

Then you will have fun exploring them together and enjoying the rhymes and free accompanying soundscapes...toot toot!

The Vehicles of the Town
ISBN (paperback): 978-3-949304-02-6
ISBN (hardcover): 978-3-949304-03-3

— *Impressum* —

© 2021 Jolas Wittler. All Rights Reserved.
Illustrated by Kama Towcik

1st Edition 2021

ISBN Paperback: 978-3-949304-10-1
ISBN Hardcover: 978-3-949304-11-8
E-Book: available without ISBN
MP3-Audiobook: downloadable www.jolaswittler.com/animalsounds
E-Mail: jo@jolaswittler.com

Curious World Books
Tobias Ebel
Wilhelm-Stein-Weg 2
22339 Hamburg
Germany

www.ingramcontent.com/pod-product-compliance
Lightning Source LLC
LaVergne TN
LVHW080500180726
843515LV00015B/15